NORTH AFRICAN COOKING

LAKELAND

Lakeland and ACP Magazines Ltd hereby exclude all liability to the extent permitted by law for any errors or omission in this book and for any loss, damage or expense (whether direct or indirect) suffered by a third party relying on any information contained in this book.

This book was created in 2012 for Lakeland by AWW Books, an imprint of Octopus Publishing Group Ltd, based on materials licensed to it by ACP Magazines Ltd, a division of PBL Media Pty Limited.

54 Park St, Sydney
GPO Box 4088, Sydney, NSW 2001
phone (02) 9282 8618; fax (02) 9267 9438
acpbooks@acpmagazines.com.au;
www.acpbooks.com.au

OCTOPUS PUBLISHING GROUP
Design – Chris Bell
Food Director – Pamela Clark

Published for Lakeland in the United Kingdom by Octopus Publishing Group Limited

Endeavour House
189 Shaftesbury Avenue
London WC2H 8JY
United Kingdom
phone + 44 (0) 207 632 5400;
fax + 44 (0) 207 632 5405
aww@octopusbooks.co.uk;
www.octopusbooks.co.uk
www.australian-womens-weekly.com

Printed and bound in China

A catalogue record for this book is available from the British Library.

ISBN 978-1-907428-75-3

© ACP Magazines Ltd 2012
ABN 18 053 273 546

The Department of Health advises that eggs should not be consumed raw. This book contains some dishes made with raw or lightly cooked eggs. It is prudent for vulnerable people such as pregnant and nursing mothers, invalids, the elderly, babies and young children to avoid uncooked or lightly cooked dishes made with eggs. Once prepared, these dishes should be kept refrigerated and used promptly.

This book also includes dishes made with nuts and nut derivatives. It is advisable for those with known allergic reactions to nuts and nut derivatives and those who may be potentially vulnerable to these allergies, such as pregnant and nursing mothers, invalids, the elderly, babies and children to avoid dishes made with nuts and nut oils. It is also prudent to check the labels of pre-prepared ingredients for the possible inclusion of nut derivatives.

Some of the recipes in this book have appeared in other publications.

NORTH AFRICAN
COOKING

Take a culinary journey through North Africa with this mouthwatering collection of over 50 recipes. Savour the distinctive flavours of dishes such as Lamb Tagine with Sweet Prunes, Aubergine Dip, Roasted Harissa Chicken and Spicy Red Couscous. And, for an delectable sweet treat, why not try Almond Rice Pudding or Watermelon & Fig Salad?

One of an exciting new series of cookbooks from Lakeland, *North African Cooking* is packed with delicious colour photos and expert hints, tips and techniques for beginners and experienced cooks alike.

With every recipe triple-tested® for perfect results, these excellent cookbooks are sure to be some of the best-loved on your kitchen bookshelf. To discover the rest of the range, together with our unrivalled selection of creative kitchenware, visit one of our friendly Lakeland stores or shop online at www.lakeland.co.uk.

CONTENTS

NORTH AFRICAN
FOOD 6

STARTERS 8

SALADS 26

TAGINES 40

ROASTS 70

ACCOMPANIMENTS 88

DESSERTS 106

GLOSSARY 124

INDEX 126

CONVERSION
CHARTS 128

NORTH AFRICAN FOOD

"Where there is food, there is no talking"
Moroccan proverb

Drawing on a history of Bedouin, Berber, Arab, Jewish, Turkish, French and Moorish influences, North African food is a colourful blend of spices and diverse ingredients that is deservedly becoming more popular.

With the Mediterranean lapping on their shores, the countries of North Africa – Algeria, Egypt, Morocco, Libya and Tunisia – share some ingredients with their northern neighbours. Heart-healthy olive oil and fresh vegetables are staples but, where the Mediterranean countries generally rely on herbs for flavour, most North African dishes are based around aromatic spices, along with ingredients such as nuts, fruits, preserved lemons and harissa.

THE TAGINE

Although used less frequently by the modern cook, the traditional tagine pot, with its distinctive, tall, cone-shaped lid is a spectacular sight when brought to the table. It is made of heavy clay or terracotta and the flat, round base with low sides serves as both a cooking and serving dish. The lid that rests inside the base during cooking is designed to trap all the condensation and return it to the bottom of pot, keeping the moisture in the food and infusing it with the spices and flavours of the dish.

CUSTOMS

Food is seen as far more than just sustenance throughout the region. It is lovingly prepared and generously shared with others. Food also has significant religious importance and specific dishes are eaten to mark religious festivals and key occasions such as marriages.

As a sign of respect for the food that God has provided and the host or hostess has served, North Africans consider it impolite to converse while eating and there is a Moroccan proverb that says: "Mâ kainsh el-kalâm cala ettacâm" ("Where there is food, there is no talking").

SOME ESSENTIAL INGREDIENTS

chickpeas Sold pre-cooked in cans or dried, this legume is prized throughout North Africa for its full, nutty flavour and crisp texture. It is the essential ingredient in hummus and is also used in tagines.

couscous The staple cereal of North Africa, made from fine semolina. The miniscule pellets are steamed over the pot in which the meat or vegetables are cooking or, for sweet couscous, steamed over water, then mixed with sugar, fruit and nuts.

harissa This is a paste made from dried chillies, garlic, olive oil and caraway seeds. It can be used as a condiment on its own, as an ingredient in sauces and dressings and as a rub for meat. Harissa is extremely hot so should be served in small amounts.

preserved lemons This is a North African and Middle Eastern speciality. The lemons are preserved, whole or cut in half, in a mixture of salt and lemon juice or oil. To use, remove and discard the flesh, rinse the rind and chop or slice into tagines, couscous or dips. Preserved lemons are particularly good with lamb dishes or sprinkled over fish.

ras el hanout With a name that translates loosely as "top of the shop", this is a blend of the best a spice merchant has to offer. Traditionally the blend may contain more than 20 spices, including allspice, cumin, paprika, fennel, caraway, cinnamon and saffron. Some versions include dried rosebuds and lavender too.

saffron Available in strands or ground form, this is expensive because it consists of the hand-gathered stigmas from crocus flowers. It colours food golden and has a bittersweet, almondy taste.

split peas These are available in both green and yellow varieties and have a sweet, strong pea flavour. They are used in soups and stews.

za'atar This blend of roasted dried thyme, oregano, marjoram, sesame seeds and sumac is found in many North African kitchens. Try it sprinkled on toast spread with ricotta or tossed with roasted potato wedges.

STARTERS

AUBERGINE DIP

2 large aubergines (1kg)
125ml olive oil
6 medium tomatoes (900g)
3 cloves garlic, crushed
4 tablespoons each coarsely
    chopped fresh flat-leaf parsley
    and coriander
1 teaspoon ground cumin
crusty bread, to serve

1 Preheat oven to 200°C/180°C fan-assisted.
2 Pierce aubergines all over with fork or skewer. Place aubergines on oiled oven tray; drizzle with 2 tablespoons of the oil. Roast aubergines, uncovered, about 50 minutes or until softened.
3 Meanwhile, place tomatoes on another oiled oven tray; drizzle with 2 tablespoons of the oil. Roast tomatoes for last 15 minutes of aubergine cooking time. Cool 20 minutes.
4 When cool enough to handle, peel aubergines and tomatoes; discard skin. Deseed tomatoes; chop tomato and aubergine flesh coarsely.
5 Heat remaining oil in large frying pan; cook garlic, aubergine and tomato, stirring occasionally, about 20 minutes or until thick. Add herbs; cook, stirring, 5 minutes. Transfer mixture to medium bowl, stir in cumin; cool 20 minutes. Season to taste. Serve with crusty bread.

prep + cook time 1 hour 20 minutes + cooling time
makes 750ml
nutritional count per tablespoon
3.3g total fat (0.5g saturated fat); 150kJ (36 cal); 0.9g carbohydrate; 0.4g protein; 0.8g fibre

RED PEPPER DIP

4 large red peppers (1.4kg)
3 cloves garlic, unpeeled
2 tablespoons olive oil
1 tablespoon red wine vinegar
1 tablespoon lemon juice
1 tablespoon finely chopped
   preserved lemon rind
½ teaspoon hot paprika
2 tablespoons finely chopped
   fresh coriander
pitta bread, to serve

1 Preheat oven to 220°C/200°C fan-assisted. Oil oven trays.
2 Quarter peppers; discard seeds and membranes. Roast, skin-side up, with garlic about 30 minutes or until skin blisters and blackens. Cover pepper and garlic with plastic or paper for 5 minutes, then peel away skins.
3 Blend or process pepper, garlic, oil, vinegar, juice, preserved lemon and paprika until smooth. Stir in coriander; season to taste.
4 Serve dip with toasted pitta bread or crusty bread.

prep + cook time 45 minutes
makes 375ml
nutritional count per tablespoon
2.2g total fat (0.3g saturated fat); 155kJ (37 cal); 2.7g carbohydrate; 1.1g protein; 0.9g fibre

BEEF & FIG CIGARS

20g butter
1 medium brown onion (150g),
   chopped finely
½ teaspoon ground cinnamon
2 cloves garlic, crushed
250g minced beef
150g finely chopped dried figs
1 tablespoon finely chopped fresh
   chives
8 sheets filo pastry
cooking-oil spray
125ml plum sauce, to serve

1 Melt butter in large frying pan; cook onion, cinnamon and garlic, stirring, until onion softens. Add beef; cook, stirring, until beef is browned. Stir in figs and chives; cool 10 minutes.

2 Meanwhile, preheat oven to 200°C/180°C fan-assisted. Oil two oven trays.

3 Spray one pastry sheet with oil; cover with a second pastry sheet. Cut lengthways into three even strips, then crossways into four even strips.

4 Place 1 rounded teaspoon of the beef mixture along the bottom of one narrow edge of pastry strip, leaving 1cm border. Fold narrow edge over beef mixture then fold in long sides; roll to enclose filling. Place cigar, seam-side down, on tray; repeat process with remaining pastry and beef mixture.

5 Spray cigars lightly with oil. Bake, uncovered, about 10 minutes or until browned lightly. Serve with plum sauce.

prep + cook time 1 hour
makes 48
nutritional count per cigar
1.2g total fat (0.5g saturated fat); 160kJ (38 cal); 5.2g carbohydrate; 1.4g protein; 0.6g fibre

VEGETARIAN CIGARS WITH HARISSA YOGURT

1 medium red pepper (200g)
1 tablespoon olive oil
1 clove garlic, crushed
1 small aubergine (230g),
   chopped finely
1 large courgette (150g),
   chopped finely
1 large tomato (220g), deseeded,
   chopped finely
1 teaspoon each ground cumin
   and sweet paprika
1 tablespoon finely chopped
   fresh mint
6 sheets filo pastry
75g butter, melted

harissa yogurt
140g natural yogurt
1 teaspoon harissa paste
1 teaspoon finely grated lemon
   rind

1 Preheat oven to 200°C/180°C fan-assisted. Oil oven trays.
2 Quarter pepper; discard seeds and membranes. Roast, skin-side up, until skin blisters and blackens. Cover pepper with plastic or paper for 5 minutes; peel away skin, then chop pepper finely.
3 Meanwhile, heat oil in large frying pan; stir garlic, aubergine, courgette and tomato about 5 minutes or until vegetables soften. Add spices; cook, stirring, about 5 minutes or until fragrant. Stir in pepper and mint; cool. Season to taste.
4 Brush 1 sheet of pastry with butter; top with a second pastry sheet. Cut layered sheets lengthways into 3 rectangles. Halve pastry rectangles crossways. Press 1 tablespoon of vegetable mixture into a log shape along one short end of each rectangle. Roll pastry over filling; fold in sides then roll up to form a cigar shape. Repeat to make a total of 18 cigars.

5 Place cigars, seam-side down, on oven trays; brush with remaining butter. Bake about 20 minutes or until browned lightly.
6 Meanwhile, make harissa yogurt; serve with cigars.

harissa yogurt Combine ingredients in small bowl.

prep + cook time 55 minutes
makes 18
nutritional count per cigar 4.8g total fat (2.5g saturated fat); 276kJ (66 cal); 4g carbohydrate; 1.3g protein; 0.8g fibre

MINTED TUNA TRIANGLES

1 tablespoon olive oil

1 medium brown onion (150g), chopped finely

4 drained anchovy fillets, chopped finely

2 teaspoons ground cumin

425g canned tuna in brine, drained, flaked

1 egg, beaten lightly

4 tablespoons finely chopped fresh flat-leaf parsley

3 tablespoons finely chopped fresh mint

12 sheets filo pastry

90g butter, melted

2 teaspoons poppy seeds

140g natural yogurt and lemon wedges, to serve

1 Heat oil in large frying pan; cook onion and anchovy, stirring, about 5 minutes or until soft. Add cumin, tuna, egg, parsley and mint; cook, stirring, about 30 seconds or until egg starts to set. Remove from heat, season to taste; cool.

2 Preheat oven to 200°C/180°C fan-assisted. Oil oven trays; line with baking parchment.

3 Brush 1 sheet of pastry with butter; top with 2 more sheets, brushing each with butter. Cut layered sheets crossways into 5 strips. Place 1 rounded tablespoon of tuna mixture at one short end of each pastry strip. Fold one corner of pastry diagonally over filling to form a triangle. Continue folding to end of strip, retaining triangle shape. Repeat to make a total of 20 triangles.

4 Place triangles on trays; brush with remaining butter, sprinkle with poppy seeds. Bake triangles about 20 minutes or until browned lightly. Serve with yogurt and lemon wedges, if you like.

prep + cook time 55 minutes
makes 20
nutritional count per triangle
5.7g total fat (2.9g saturated fat); 393kJ (94 cal); 5.1g carbohydrate; 5.4g protein; 0.4g fibre

GOAT'S CHEESE WITH CHICKPEAS & PEPPERS

2 large green peppers (700g)
2 large red peppers (700g)
2 tablespoons olive oil
1 medium red onion (170g),
    sliced thinly
2 cloves garlic, crushed
1 teaspoon ground cumin
½ teaspoon hot paprika
400g canned chickpeas, rinsed,
    drained
2 teaspoons finely grated lemon
    rind
1 tablespoon lemon juice
4 tablespoons coarsely chopped
    fresh flat-leaf parsley
60g soft goat's cheese
soft bread rolls, to serve

1 Preheat oven to 200°C/180°C fan-assisted. Oil oven trays.
2 Quarter peppers; discard seeds and membranes. Roast, skin-side up, until skin blisters and blackens. Cover pepper with plastic or paper for 5 minutes; peel away skin, then slice pepper thinly.
3 Heat oil in large frying pan; stir onion and garlic, until onion softens. Add spices and half the chickpeas; cook, stirring, about 2 minutes or until fragrant. Add pepper; cook, stirring, until heated through. Remove from heat; stir in rind, juice and parsley. Cool.
4 Meanwhile, coarsely mash remaining chickpeas with cheese in medium bowl.
5 Stir pepper mixture into cheese mixture; season to taste. Serve dip with soft bread rolls or toasted pitta bread.

prep + cook time 50 minutes
makes 750ml
nutritional count per tablespoon
1.5g total fat (0.3g saturated fat); 121kJ (29 cal); 2.3g carbohydrate; 1.3g protein; 0.8g fibre

ROSEWATER & SESAME CHICKEN DRUMSTICKS

20 chicken drumsticks (1.4kg)
2 tablespoons brown sugar
80ml rosewater
1 tablespoon olive oil
½ teaspoon ground allspice
2 teaspoons sesame seeds

1 Using small sharp knife pierce chicken all over. Combine chicken, sugar, rosewater, oil and spice in large bowl. Cover; refrigerate 3 hours or overnight.
2 Preheat oven to 220°C/200°C fan-assisted.
3 Place chicken on oiled wire rack over large baking dish; pour over any remaining marinade, sprinkle with seeds. Roast chicken, uncovered, basting with pan juices occasionally, about 30 minutes or until cooked through.

prep + cook time 35 minutes + refrigeration time
makes 20
nutritional count per drumstick
5.3g total fat (1.4g saturated fat); 330kJ (79 cal); 1.3g carbohydrate; 6.8g protein; 0g fibre

LAMB KEBABS WITH YOGURT & PITTA BREAD

500g minced lamb
1 egg
1 small brown onion, finely
  chopped
2 tablespoons finely chopped
  fresh flat-leaf parsley
1 clove garlic, crushed
2 teaspoons each ground
  cinnamon and sweet paprika
½ teaspoon cayenne pepper
140g natural yogurt, lemon
  wedges and pitta bread,
  to serve

1 Combine minced lamb mince,
egg, chopped onion, parsley,
garlic, cinnamon, sweet paprika
and cayenne pepper in bowl.
2 Form lamb mixture into 16
sausage shapes. Thread onto 16
small bamboo skewers or strong
toothpicks; flatten slightly.
3 Cook on heated oiled grill plate
(or grill or barbecue) until browned
and cooked as desired.
4 Serve kebabs with yogurt,
lemon wedges and pitta bread.

prep + cook time 30 minutes
makes 16
nutritional count per serving
10.8g total fat (4.8g saturated
fat); 1004kJ (240 cal); 5.6g
carbohydrate; 29.2g protein;
0.4g fibre

SALADS

CUCUMBER & FETA SALAD WITH ZA'ATAR

1 cucumber (260g), peeled,
  sliced thinly
90g feta cheese
2 tablespoons finely chopped
  fresh mint
1 tablespoon lemon juice
1 tablespoon olive oil
2 teaspoons za'atar

1 Arrange cucumber on large serving platter.
2 Combine cheese and mint in small bowl; sprinkle cheese mixture over cucumber. Drizzle with juice and oil, then sprinkle with za'atar.

prep time 10 minutes
serves 4
nutritional count per serving
9.9g total fat (4.1g saturated fat); 468kJ (112 cal); 1.2g carbohydrate; 4.3g protein; 0.7g fibre

SWEET CUCUMBER & ORANGE SALAD

2 large oranges (600g)
1 large cucumber (400g)
2 large handfuls fresh mint leaves

honey lemon dressing
60ml avocado oil
1 tablespoon finely grated
   lemon rind
1 tablespoon lemon juice
2 teaspoons honey

1 Make honey lemon dressing.
2 Segment oranges over small bowl; reserve juice.
3 Use vegetable peeler to cut cucumber into thin ribbons. Place cucumber in medium bowl with mint, orange segments, reserved juice and dressing; toss gently to combine. Season to taste.

honey lemon dressing Place ingredients in screw-top jar; shake well.

prep time 20 minutes
serves 4
nutritional count per serving
14.3g total fat (1.7g saturated fat); 840kJ (201 cal); 13.5g carbohydrate; 2.6g protein; 4.6g fibre

tip Traditionally served as an accompaniment to spicy dishes, this recipe would also make a great light vegetarian starter.

SALAD OF HERBS

60g rocket leaves

6 tablespoons each fresh flat-leaf
   parsley and coriander leaves

230g watercress

½ small red onion (50g), sliced
   thinly

55g pitted mixed olives, chopped
   coarsely

preserved lemon dressing

1 clove garlic, crushed

1 tablespoon olive oil

¼ teaspoon sweet paprika

2 tablespoons lemon juice

1 tablespoon finely chopped
   preserved lemon rind

1 Make preserved lemon dressing.
2 Combine ingredients and
dressing in large bowl; season
to taste.

preserved lemon dressing Place
ingredients in screw-top jar; shake
well.

prep time 15 minutes
serves 4
nutritional count per serving
5.3g total fat (0.7g saturated fat);
339kJ (81 cal); 3.9g carbohydrate;
2.6g protein; 3.5g fibre

ROASTED PEPPER & BEETROOT SALAD

500g baby beetroot
1 small red pepper (150g)
1 small orange pepper (150g)
1 small yellow pepper (150g)
cooking-oil spray
½ small red onion (50g), chopped
 finely
1 tablespoon finely chopped fresh
 flat-leaf parsley
1 tablespoon thinly sliced
 preserved lemon rind
1 tablespoon lemon juice

1 Preheat oven to 220°C/200°C fan-assisted.

2 Trim leaves from beetroot; wrap each beetroot in foil, place on oven tray. Place peppers on baking-parchment-lined oven tray; spray with oil. Roast beetroot and peppers about 30 minutes or until beetroot are tender and peppers have blistered and blackened.

3 Cool beetroot 10 minutes then peel and quarter. Cover peppers with plastic or paper for 5 minutes. Quarter peppers; discard seeds and membranes. Peel away skin, then halve each quarter lengthways.

4 Arrange beetroot and pepper on large serving platter. Sprinkle with onion, parsley and preserved lemon; drizzle with juice.

prep + cook time 50 minutes
serves 4
nutritional count per serving
1.6g total fat (0.2g saturated fat); 397kJ (95 cal); 13.9g carbohydrate; 3.9g protein; 4.8g fibre

CARROT, RAISIN & HERB SALAD

1.2kg baby carrots, trimmed
1 teaspoon each ground cumin
  and sweet paprika
½ teaspoon ground cinnamon
60ml olive oil
60ml orange juice
2 tablespoons lemon juice
50g raisins
1 large handful coarsely chopped
  fresh flat-leaf parsley
3 tablespoons fresh mint leaves

1 Preheat oven to 200°C/180°C fan-assisted.

2 Combine carrots, spices and half the oil in large shallow baking dish; roast, uncovered, about 15 minutes or until carrots are tender. Cool 20 minutes.

3 Meanwhile, make dressing by combining juices, raisins, remaining oil and half the parsley in large jug; season to taste.

4 Serve carrots drizzled with dressing; sprinkle with mint leaves and remaining parsley.

prep + cook time 30 minutes + cooling time
serves 6
nutritional count per serving
9.4g total fat (1.3g saturated fat); 698kJ (167 cal); 16.2g carbohydrate; 1.9g protein; 5.9g fibre

RADISH & CUCUMBER CHOPPED SALAD

4 trimmed red radishes (60g), sliced thinly
1 cucumber (260g), peeled, chopped finely
1 small red onion (100g), sliced thinly
½ teaspoon sea salt
1 clove garlic, crushed
2 tablespoons lemon juice
60ml olive oil
6 tablespoons coarsely chopped fresh mint
60g rocket leaves
2 medium vine-ripened tomatoes (300g), chopped finely
30g pitted small black olives

1 Place radish, cucumber and onion in salad bowl, sprinkle with salt; leave to stand for 5 minutes.
2 Pour combined garlic, juice and oil over vegetables in bowl; toss gently to combine. Cover; refrigerate 2 hours.
3 Just before serving, stir in mint, rocket and tomatoes. Serve salad topped with olives.

prep time 15 minutes + refrigeration time
serves 6
nutritional count per serving
9.4g total fat (1.3g saturated fat); 468kJ (112 cal); 4.5g carbohydrate; 1.5g protein; 2g fibre

TAGINES

LAMB, ARTICHOKE & PEPPER TAGINE

1kg boned lamb shoulder, chopped coarsely
2 teaspoons each ground ginger and cinnamon
1 teaspoon hot paprika
2 tablespoons olive oil
1 large red onion (300g), sliced thickly
3 cloves garlic, crushed
375ml beef stock
340g bottled marinated artichoke hearts, drained, halved
80g drained, thinly sliced bottled roasted red pepper
40g thinly sliced preserved lemon rind
3 tablespoons coarsely chopped fresh flat-leaf parsley

1 Combine lamb and half the combined spices in large bowl.
2 Heat half the oil in tagine or flameproof casserole dish; cook lamb, in batches, until browned. Remove from tagine.
3 Heat remaining oil in same tagine; cook onion and garlic, stirring, until soft. Add remaining spices; cook, stirring, about 1 minute or until fragrant. Return lamb to tagine with stock; bring to the boil. Reduce heat; simmer, covered, about 50 minutes or until lamb is tender.
4 Add artichokes, pepper and rind; simmer, uncovered, until heated through. Season to taste.
5 Sprinkle tagine with parsley before serving.

prep + cook time 1 hour 30 minutes
serves 6
nutritional count per serving 16.3g total fat (5.5g saturated fat); 1321kJ (316 cal); 4.6g carbohydrate; 36g protein; 2.7g fibre

LAMB TAGINE WITH SWEET PRUNES

1kg boned lamb shoulder,
  chopped coarsely
80ml olive oil
2 medium red onions (340g),
  grated coarsely
4 cloves garlic, crushed
1 teaspoon each ground ginger
  and sweet paprika
¼ teaspoon each dried chilli
  flakes and saffron threads
800g canned chopped tomatoes
4 x 5cm strips orange rind
2 cinnamon sticks
6 tablespoons coarsely chopped
  fresh coriander

sweet prunes
18 pitted prunes (145g)
90g honey
2 tablespoons water

1 Combine lamb, oil, onion, garlic
and spices in large bowl. Cover;
refrigerate 3 hours or overnight.
2 Preheat oven to 180°C/160°C
fan-assisted.
3 Heat oiled tagine or flameproof
casserole dish on stove top; cook
lamb, in batches, until browned.
4 Return lamb to tagine with
undrained tomatoes, rind,
cinnamon sticks and half the
coriander; bring to the boil.
5 Cover tagine, transfer to oven;
cook about 1½ hours or until lamb
is tender, season to taste.
6 Meanwhile, make sweet prunes.
7 Serve tagine with sweet prunes;
sprinkle with remaining coriander.

sweet prunes Bring ingredients
to the boil in small saucepan.
Reduce heat; simmer, uncovered,
10 minutes.

prep + cook time 1 hour
50 minutes + refrigeration time
serves 6
nutritional count per serving
22.1g total fat (6.2g saturated
fat); 1969kJ (471 cal); 30.5g
carbohydrate; 35.9g protein;
4.6g fibre

Lamb tagine with ras el hanout

750g boned lamb shoulder, chopped coarsely
2 tablespoons ras el hanout
60ml olive oil
8 baby new potatoes (320g), halved
2 small leeks (400g), sliced thinly
1 litre beef consommé
2 tablespoons finely chopped fresh flat-leaf parsley

1 Combine lamb, ras el hanout and 1 tablespoon of the oil in large bowl. Cover, refrigerate 3 hours or overnight.
2 Preheat oven to 200°C/180°C fan-assisted.
3 Heat 1 tablespoon of the remaining oil in tagine or flameproof casserole dish on stove top; cook lamb, in batches, until browned. Remove from tagine.
4 Heat remaining oil in same tagine; cook potato and leek, stirring, until potatoes are browned lightly and leek softens. Return lamb to tagine with consommé; bring to the boil.
5 Cover tagine, transfer to oven; cook about 45 minutes or until lamb is tender. Remove from oven; stir in parsley. Season to taste.

prep + cook time 1 hour + refrigeration time
serves 4
nutritional count per serving 25.7g total fat (7.5g saturated fat); 2023kJ (484 cal); 16.9g carbohydrate; 44.2g protein; 4.7g fibre
tip You can use canned consommé for a good flavour, but if you prefer, use stock instead.

MEATBALL TAGINE WITH EGGS

500g minced beef
1 clove garlic, crushed
3 tablespoons finely chopped
  fresh mint
2 tablespoons finely chopped
  fresh coriander
1 teaspoon each ground
  coriander and cinnamon
2 teaspoons ground cumin
½ teaspoon chilli powder
1 tablespoon olive oil
1 medium brown onion (150g),
  chopped finely
4 large tomatoes (880g), chopped
  coarsely
pinch saffron threads
4 eggs
6 tablespoons fresh coriander
  leaves

1 Combine minced beef, garlic, mint, chopped coriander, ground coriander, cinnamon, half the cumin and half the chilli in large bowl; season. Roll level tablespoons of mixture into balls.
2 Heat oil in tagine or large frying pan; cook meatballs, in batches, until browned. Remove from tagine.
3 Cook onion in same tagine, stirring, until softened. Add tomato, saffron and remaining cumin and chilli; bring to the boil. Reduce heat; simmer, uncovered, about 15 minutes or until tomatoes soften.
4 Return meatballs to tagine; simmer, uncovered, about 10 minutes or until meatballs are cooked and sauce thickens slightly. Season to taste. Carefully crack eggs into tagine; simmer, covered, about 5 minutes or until eggs are barely set. Sprinkle tagine with coriander leaves.

prep + cook time 1 hour
serves 4
nutritional count per serving
20.2g total fat (7.1g saturated fat); 1488kJ (356 cal); 6.6g carbohydrate; 35.3g protein; 3.5g fibre

BEEF & AUBERGINE TAGINE

2 tablespoons olive oil

625g braising steak, chopped coarsely

1 medium brown onion (150g), chopped coarsely

2 cloves garlic, crushed

2 teaspoons ground coriander

1 teaspoon each ground ginger, cumin and sweet paprika

125ml beef stock

3 medium tomatoes (450g), chopped coarsely

3 baby aubergines (180g), sliced thickly

1 Heat half the oil in tagine or large saucepan; cook beef, in batches, until browned. Remove from tagine.

2 Cook onion in same tagine, stirring, until softened. Add garlic and spices; cook, stirring, until fragrant. Return beef to tagine with stock and tomato; bring to the boil. Reduce heat; simmer, covered, 45 minutes. Uncover; simmer 30 minutes or until beef is tender and tagine thickens.

3 Meanwhile, heat remaining oil in medium frying pan; cook aubergine, stirring, about 10 minutes or until browned and tender.

4 Stir aubergine into tagine; season to taste.

prep + cook time 1 hour 30 minutes
serves 4
nutritional count per serving
21.2g total fat (5.9g saturated fat); 1538kJ (368 cal); 5.7g carbohydrate; 37.3g protein; 3.1g fibre

BEEF, RAISIN & ALMOND TAGINE

1 tablespoon olive oil
625g braising steak, chopped coarsely
1 medium brown onion (150g), chopped coarsely
2 cloves garlic, crushed
2 teaspoons ras el hanout
½ teaspoon each ground ginger and ground cinnamon
1 dried bay leaf
250ml beef stock
35g coarsely chopped raisins
40g blanched almonds, roasted
lemon wedges, to serve

1 Heat oil in tagine or large frying pan; cook beef, in batches, until browned. Remove from tagine.
2 Cook onion in same tagine, stirring, until softened. Add garlic, spices and bay leaf; cook, stirring, until fragrant. Return beef to pan with stock; bring to the boil. Reduce heat; simmer, covered, 1 hour. Add raisins; simmer, uncovered, about 15 minutes or until beef is tender and tagine thickens. Stir in nuts, season to taste; accompany with lemon wedges.

prep + cook time 1 hour 30 minutes
serves 4
nutritional count per serving
22.1g total fat (5.6g saturated fat); 1630kJ (390 cal); 9.2g carbohydrate; 38.3g protein; 2.1g fibre

CHICKEN TAGINE WITH OLIVES & LEMON

2kg whole chicken
2 teaspoons each ground ginger, cumin and ground coriander
1 tablespoon olive oil
1 large brown onion (200g), sliced thickly
3 cloves garlic, crushed
¼ teaspoon ground turmeric
pinch saffron threads
250ml water
250ml chicken stock
625g baby new potatoes, halved
375g pumpkin or butternut squash, unpeeled, cut into wedges
120g pitted green olives
2 tablespoons thinly sliced preserved lemon rind
2 tablespoons lemon juice
6 tablespoons coarsely chopped fresh flat-leaf parsley
3 tablespoons coarsely chopped fresh coriander

1 Rinse chicken under cold water; pat dry inside and out with absorbent paper. Using kitchen scissors, cut along both sides of backbone; discard backbone. Press down on breastbone to flatten out chicken. Combine half the combined ground ginger, cumin and coriander in small bowl; rub mixture over chicken.

2 Preheat oven to 220°C/200°C fan-assisted.

3 Heat oil in tagine or flameproof casserole dish on stove top; cook chicken until browned all over. Remove from tagine. Reserve 1 tablespoon pan drippings; discard remainder.

4 Heat reserved pan drippings in same tagine; cook onion and garlic, stirring, until soft. Add turmeric and saffron, and remaining ginger, cumin and coriander; cook, stirring, about 1 minute or until fragrant. Add the water, stock, potatoes and pumpkin; top with chicken. Bring to the boil.

5 Cover tagine, transfer to oven; cook about 1¼ hours or until chicken is cooked.

6 Stir olives, preserved lemon and juice into sauce; season to taste. Serve tagine sprinkled with herbs.

prep + cook time 2 hours
serves 6
nutritional count per serving
34.5g total fat (9.6g saturated fat); 2316kJ (554 cal); 20.1g carbohydrate; 38.4g protein; 4.4g fibre

CHICKEN TAGINE WITH PRUNES & HONEY

2 teaspoons sesame seeds
30g butter
80g blanched almonds
1.5kg whole chicken
60ml olive oil
1 medium brown onion (150g),
    sliced thinly
2 teaspoons ground ginger
1 teaspoon ground cinnamon
¼ teaspoon ground turmeric
pinch saffron threads
375ml water
175g honey
125g pitted prunes
1 tablespoon thinly sliced
    preserved lemon rind

1 Dry-fry sesame seeds in tagine or large frying pan until browned lightly. Remove from tagine.
2 Melt butter in same tagine; cook almonds, stirring, until browned lightly. Remove from tagine.
3 Rinse chicken under cold water; pat dry inside and out with absorbent paper. Using kitchen scissors, cut chicken into eight pieces.
4 Heat oil in same tagine; cook chicken, in batches, until browned. Remove from tagine. Reserve 1 tablespoon pan juices; discard remainder.
5 Heat reserved pan juices in same tagine; cook onion, stirring, until soft. Add spices; cook, stirring about 1 minute or until fragrant. Return chicken to tagine and toss to coat in onion mixture. Add the water; bring to the boil. Reduce heat; simmer, covered, about 30 minutes or until chicken is cooked.
6 Remove chicken from tagine; cover to keep warm. Add honey and prunes to tagine; simmer, uncovered, about 10 minutes or until sauce thickens slightly.

7 Return chicken to tagine; cook, covered, until heated through.
8 Serve tagine sprinkled with sesame seeds, almonds and preserved lemon.

prep + cook time 1 hour 15 minutes
serves 8
nutritional count per serving
31.2g total fat (8.1g saturated fat); 1956kJ (468 cal); 24.6g carbohydrate; 21.6g protein; 2.5g fibre

CHICKEN TAGINE WITH FIGS & WALNUTS

55g coarsely chopped walnuts
4 chicken drumsticks (600g)
4 chicken thighs (800g)
2 teaspoons cumin seeds
2 teaspoons each ground ginger
   and cinnamon
1 tablespoon olive oil
1 large red onion (300g), sliced
   thickly
pinch saffron threads
375ml chicken stock
1 tablespoon honey
6 medium fresh figs (360g),
   halved
1 teaspoon granulated sugar
45g baby spinach leaves
3 tablespoons finely chopped
   fresh flat-leaf parsley

1 Dry-fry nuts in tagine or flameproof casserole dish until browned lightly. Remove from tagine.
2 Combine chicken and cumin seeds with half the ginger and half the cinnamon in large bowl.
3 Heat oil in same tagine; cook chicken, in batches, until browned. Remove from tagine. Reserve 1 tablespoon pan juices; discard remainder.
4 Heat reserved pan juices in same tagine; cook onion, stirring, until soft. Add saffron and remaining ginger and cinnamon; cook, stirring, about 2 minutes or until fragrant. Return chicken to tagine with stock; bring to the boil. Reduce heat; simmer, covered, about 30 minutes or until chicken is cooked.
5 Remove chicken from tagine; cover to keep warm. Add honey to tagine; simmer, uncovered, about 10 minutes or until sauce is browned and thickened slightly.

6 Meanwhile, preheat grill. Place figs, cut-side up, on a baking-parchment-lined oven tray; sprinkle with sugar. Cook under grill about 5 minutes or until browned lightly.
7 Return chicken to tagine with spinach; simmer, covered, until heated through. Season to taste.
8 Serve tagine topped with figs; sprinkle with nuts and parsley.

prep + cook time 1 hour 10 minutes
serves 6
nutritional count per serving
30.2g total fat (7.5g saturated fat); 1873kJ (448 cal); 12.9g carbohydrate; 30.5g protein; 3.1g fibre

CHILLI FISH TAGINE

4 x 200g white fish fillets, skin on
1 tablespoon finely grated lemon
   rind
2 teaspoons dried chilli flakes
2 cloves garlic, crushed
1 tablespoon olive oil
30g butter
2 baby fennel bulbs (260g),
   trimmed, cut into wedges
150g green beans, halved
   lengthways
50g raisins
250ml dry white wine
pinch saffron threads
45g roasted unsalted shelled
   pistachios, to serve

1 Combine fish, rind, chilli, garlic and oil in large bowl. Cover; refrigerate 3 hours or overnight.
2 Melt butter in tagine or large frying pan; cook fennel, stirring, until browned lightly. Add beans, raisins, wine and saffron; top with fish. Bring to the boil. Reduce heat; simmer, covered, about 15 minutes or until fish is cooked as desired. Season to taste.
3 Serve tagine sprinkled with nuts.

prep + cook time 30 minutes + refrigeration time
serves 4
nutritional count per serving
21.1g total fat (6.7g saturated fat); 1956kJ (468 cal); 13.1g carbohydrate; 44.8g protein; 4g fibre
tips You can use any firm white fish fillets for this recipe. Fish or chicken stock can be used instead of wine.

SPICY PRAWN & TOMATO TAGINE

1 tablespoon olive oil

1 medium brown onion (150g), chopped finely

3 cloves garlic, crushed

1 teaspoon each ground ginger and cumin

¼ teaspoon chilli powder

pinch saffron threads

1kg tomatoes, chopped coarsely

1.5kg uncooked king prawns

3 tablespoons each finely chopped fresh flat-leaf parsley and coriander

30g finely chopped roasted unsalted shelled pistachios

1 tablespoon finely chopped preserved lemon rind

1 Heat oil in tagine or flameproof casserole dish; cook onion and garlic, stirring, until onion softens. Add spices; cook, stirring, about 1 minute or until fragrant. Add tomato; cook, stirring, about 5 minutes or until tomato softens. Bring to the boil. Reduce heat; simmer, stirring occasionally, about 10 minutes or until sauce thickens slightly.

2 Meanwhile, shell and devein prawns leaving tails intact. Add prawns to tagine; cook, covered, stirring occasionally, about 5 minutes or until prawns are changed in colour. Season to taste.

3 Combine herbs, nuts and preserved lemon in small bowl.

4 Serve tagine sprinkled with herb mixture.

prep + cook time 40 minutes
serves 6
nutritional count per serving
6.6g total fat (0.9g saturated fat); 857kJ (205 cal); 5.5g carbohydrate; 28.8g protein; 3.2g fibre

WHITE BEAN & LENTIL TAGINE

1 tablespoon olive oil

1 medium brown onion (150g), chopped coarsely

2 cloves garlic, crushed

2.5cm piece fresh ginger (15g), cut into matchsticks

1 teaspoon harissa

800g canned whole peeled tomatoes, chopped coarsely

1 medium red pepper (200g), chopped coarsely

125ml water

400g canned white beans, rinsed, drained

400g canned brown lentils, rinsed, drained

3 tablespoons finely chopped fresh mint

3 tablespoons finely chopped fresh flat-leaf parsley, to serve

1 Heat oil in tagine or large frying pan; cook onion, stirring, until softened. Add garlic, ginger and harissa; cook, stirring, about 1 minute or until fragrant.

2 Add undrained tomatoes, pepper, the water, beans and lentils; bring to the boil. Reduce heat; simmer, uncovered, about 15 minutes or until tagine thickens. Remove from heat; stir in mint, season to taste.

3 Serve tagine sprinkled with parsley.

prep + cook time 40 minutes
serves 4
nutritional count per serving
5.8g total fat (0.8g saturated fat); 865kJ (207 cal); 23.8g carbohydrate; 10.6g protein; 10.2g fibre

tip We used cannellini beans in this recipe but you can use any canned white beans you like.

SWEET & SPICY VEGETABLE TAGINE

2 tablespoons olive oil

1 medium brown onion (150g), sliced thinly

5cm piece fresh ginger (25g), grated

2 cloves garlic, crushed

2 teaspoons each ground coriander and cumin

1 teaspoon sweet paprika

500g pumpkin or butternut squash, chopped coarsely

1 medium sweet potato (400g), chopped coarsely

2 small parsnips (240g), chopped coarsely

500ml vegetable stock

400g canned chopped tomatoes

2 tablespoons honey

8 small yellow patty pan squash (185g), halved

375g baby carrots, trimmed

50g raisins

2 tablespoons finely chopped fresh flat-leaf parsley

20g flaked almonds, roasted

1 Heat oil in tagine or flameproof casserole dish; cook onion, stirring, until softened. Add ginger, garlic and spices; cook, stirring, about 1 minute or until fragrant.

2 Add pumpkin, sweet potato, parsnip, stock, undrained tomatoes and honey; bring to the boil. Reduce heat; simmer, covered, 15 minutes. Add squash and carrots; simmer, uncovered, 20 minutes or until vegetables are tender, season to taste.

3 Stir in raisins and parsley; sprinkle with nuts.

prep + cook time 55 minutes
serves 8
nutritional count per serving
6.8g total fat (1g saturated fat); 857kJ (205 cal); 28.4g carbohydrate; 5.4g protein; 5.3g fibre

VEGETABLE TAGINE WITH SPLIT PEAS

2 tablespoons olive oil

1 large red onion (300g), sliced thinly

150g yellow split peas

2 cloves garlic, crushed

5cm piece fresh ginger (25g), grated

3 teaspoons ground coriander

2 teaspoons each ground cumin and sweet paprika

1 teaspoon caraway seeds

1 litre vegetable stock

400g canned chopped tomatoes

750g butternut squash, cut into 2cm pieces

350g yellow patty pan squash, quartered

200g green beans, trimmed, halved widthways

125ml water

6 tablespoons coarsely chopped fresh coriander, to serve

1 Heat oil in tagine or large saucepan; cook onion, stirring, until softened. Add peas, garlic, ginger, spices and seeds; cook, stirring, until fragrant.

2 Add stock and undrained tomatoes; bring to the boil. Reduce heat; simmer, uncovered, stirring occasionally, 15 minutes. Add butternut squash; simmer about 15 minutes or until peas are tender. Stir in patty pan squash, beans and the water, cover; cook about 5 minutes or until vegetables are tender, season to taste.

3 Serve tagine sprinkled with chopped coriander.

prep + cook time 1 hour
serves 6
nutritional count per serving
8.3g total fat (1.6g saturated fat); 1070kJ (256 cal); 27.8g carbohydrate; 13.5g protein; 7.9g fibre

ROASTS

SPICED LAMB ROAST WITH FIGS & HONEY

3 cloves garlic, chopped finely

4cm piece fresh ginger (20g), grated

2 fresh long red chillies, chopped finely

4 tablespoons each finely chopped fresh coriander and flat-leaf parsley

2 teaspoons each ground coriander and cumin

60ml olive oil

2kg leg of lamb

9 medium fresh figs (540g), halved

2 tablespoons honey

1 Preheat oven to 180°C/160°C fan-assisted.

2 Combine garlic, ginger, chilli, herbs, spices and oil in small bowl.

3 Rub herb mixture all over lamb; season. Place lamb in oiled large baking dish; roast, uncovered, 1¼ hours.

4 Add figs to dish; drizzle honey over figs and lamb. Roast 15 minutes or until lamb is cooked as desired. Cover lamb; stand 10 minutes, before slicing.

5 Serve sliced lamb with figs.

prep + cook time 1 hour 50 minutes

serves 6

nutritional count per serving 24.3g total fat (8.4g saturated fat); 2115kJ (506 cal); 15.6g carbohydrate; 55.6g protein; 2.9g fibre

tip Make double the herb rub mixture and toss through steamed couscous to make a good accompaniment to the lamb.

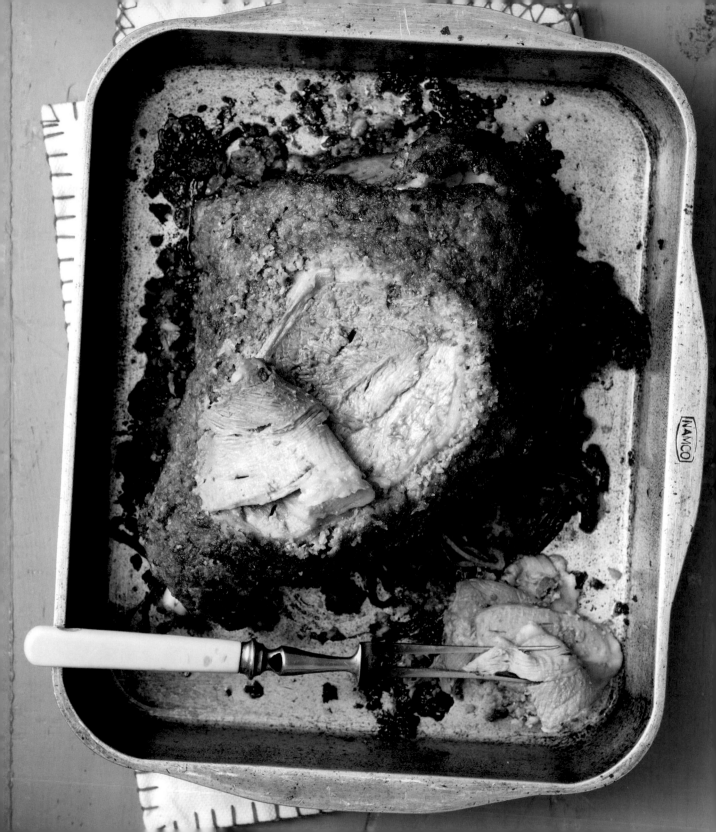

ALMOND HARISSA ROAST LAMB

4 cloves garlic, halved
1 tablespoon harissa
2 tablespoons coarsely chopped
   fresh flat-leaf parsley
2 large brown onions (600g),
   sliced thinly
125ml olive oil
60g ground almonds
1.8kg leg of lamb

1 Preheat oven to 220°C/200°C fan-assisted.
2 Blend or process garlic, harissa, parsley, half the onion and 80ml of the oil until smooth. Transfer mixture to medium bowl, stir in ground almonds.
3 Make deep cuts in lamb to the bone, at 2.5cm intervals. Rub almond mixture all over lamb.
4 Place remaining onion in oiled large baking dish; top with lamb. Drizzle with remaining oil; season. Roast lamb, uncovered, 25 minutes.
5 Reduce oven to 160°C/140°C fan-assisted.
6 Roast lamb a further 1 hour or until cooked as desired. Remove lamb from oven, cover loosely with foil; stand 20 minutes before slicing.

prep + cook time 1 hour 45 minutes + standing time
serves 6
nutritional count per serving
38g total fat (9.5g saturated fat); 2424kJ (580 cal); 6.7g carbohydrate; 52.2g protein; 2.8g fibre

SLOW-ROASTED SPICED LAMB SHOULDER

2 teaspoons fennel seeds
1 teaspoon each ground
  cinnamon, ginger and cumin
¼ teaspoon chilli powder
2 tablespoons olive oil
1.2kg lamb shoulder, shank intact
2 cloves garlic, sliced thinly
6 baby brown onions (150g)
375g baby carrots, trimmed
250ml water
green beans, to serve

1 Preheat oven to 180°C/160°C fan-assisted.
2 Dry-fry spices in small frying pan until fragrant. Combine spices and half the oil in small bowl.
3 Using sharp knife, score lamb at 2.5cm intervals; push garlic into cuts. Rub lamb all over with spice mixture, season.
4 Heat remaining oil in large flameproof dish; cook lamb, turning, until browned all over. Remove lamb from dish.
5 Meanwhile, peel onions, leaving root ends intact. Add onions to dish; cook, stirring, until browned.
6 Add carrots and the water to dish, bring to the boil; top with lamb, cover loosely with foil. Transfer to oven; roast 1½ hours.
7 Reduce oven to 160°C/140°C fan-assisted.
8 Uncover lamb; roast a further 1½ hours or until lamb is tender. Cover lamb; stand 10 minutes, then slice thinly. Strain pan juices into small heatproof jug.
9 Serve lamb with onions, carrots and pan juices; accompany with steamed green beans, if you like.

prep + cook time 3 hours 30 minutes
serves 4
nutritional count per serving
21.9g total fat (7.3g saturated fat); 1722kJ (412 cal); 6.5g carbohydrate; 45.7g protein; 3.1g fibre

CITRUS CHICKEN WITH ORANGE & PISTACHIO COUSCOUS

3 cloves garlic, crushed
1 tablespoon finely chopped fresh oregano
60ml lemon juice
170g orange marmalade
2 fresh small red chillies, chopped finely
4 x 200g chicken breast fillets
500ml chicken stock
400g couscous
2 medium oranges (480g)
2 spring onions, sliced thinly
45g roasted unsalted shelled pistachios, chopped coarsely

1 Preheat oven to 200°C/180°C fan-assisted. Oil oven tray; line with baking parchment.

2 Combine garlic, oregano, juice, marmalade and chilli in medium bowl; add chicken, turn to coat in mixture.

3 Drain chicken, reserve marmalade mixture. Cook chicken on heated oiled grill plate (or grill or barbecue) until browned both sides. Place chicken on oven tray, drizzle with reserved marmalade mixture; roast in oven, uncovered, about 10 minutes or until chicken is cooked through.

4 Meanwhile, bring stock to the boil in medium saucepan. Combine couscous with hot stock in large heatproof bowl, cover; stand about 5 minutes or until liquid is absorbed, fluffing with fork occasionally. Segment oranges over couscous; stir in onion and nuts, season to taste.

5 Serve couscous topped with chicken.

prep + cook time 25 minutes
serves 4
nutritional count per serving
18g total fat (4.4g saturated fat); 3620kJ (866 cal); 113g carbohydrate; 60.4g protein; 4.3g fibre

CHICKEN WITH COUSCOUS STUFFING

1.6kg whole chicken
20g butter, melted
20 baby vine tomatoes (400g)
1 tablespoon olive oil

couscous stuffing
1 teaspoon olive oil
1 medium brown onion (150g),
  chopped finely
375ml chicken stock
60ml olive oil, extra
1 tablespoon finely grated
  lemon rind
60ml lemon juice
200g couscous
70g roasted slivered almonds
140g pitted dried dates, chopped
  finely
1 teaspoon each ground
  cinnamon and smoked paprika
1 egg, beaten lightly

1 Make couscous stuffing.
2 Preheat oven to 200°C/180°C fan-assisted.
3 Rinse chicken under cold water; pat dry inside and out with absorbent paper. Tuck wing tips under chicken. Trim skin around neck; secure neck flap to underside of chicken with skewers. Fill large cavity loosely with couscous stuffing; tie legs together with kitchen string.
4 Half fill large baking dish with water; place chicken on oiled wire rack over dish. Brush chicken all over with butter, season; roast, uncovered, 15 minutes. Reduce oven to 180°C/160°C fan-assisted; roast, uncovered, about 1½ hours or until cooked through. Remove chicken from rack; cover, stand 20 minutes.
5 Meanwhile, place tomatoes on oven tray; drizzle with oil. Roast, uncovered, about 20 minutes or until softened and browned lightly.
6 Serve chicken with tomatoes.

couscous stuffing Heat oil in small frying pan; cook onion, stirring, until soft. Combine stock, extra oil, rind and juice in medium saucepan; bring to the boil. Remove from heat. Add couscous, cover; stand about 5 minutes or until liquid is absorbed, fluffing with fork occasionally. Stir in onion, nuts, dates, spices and egg; season to taste.

prep + cook time 2 hours 50 minutes + standing time
serves 4
nutritional count per serving
67.4g total fat (16.7g saturated fat); 4565kJ (1092 cal); 67.8g carbohydrate; 54.9g protein; 7.2g fibre

ROASTED HARISSA CHICKEN

1.8kg whole chicken
225g harissa
1 large carrot (180g), halved
   lengthways
1 large red onion (300g),
   quartered
2 stalks celery (300g), trimmed
10 sprigs (20g) fresh lemon thyme
1 medium garlic bulb (70g),
   halved crossways
2 tablespoons olive oil

1 Rinse chicken under cold water; pat dry inside and out with absorbent paper. Tuck wing tips under chicken. Brush harissa all over chicken; tie legs together with kitchen string. Cover; refrigerate 3 hours or overnight.
2 Preheat oven to 200°C/180°C fan-assisted.
3 Combine remaining ingredients in large shallow baking dish; top with chicken, season.
4 Roast chicken about 1¼ hours or until chicken is cooked through. Cover; stand 10 minutes before serving.

prep + cook time 1 hour 35 minutes + refrigeration time
serves 4
nutritional count per serving 47.4g total fat (13g saturated fat); 2968kJ (710 cal); 19.6g carbohydrate; 48.1g protein; 8.4g fibre

ROAST TROUT WITH ORANGE ALMOND FILLING

45g butter

1 small red onion (100g), chopped finely

1 stalk celery (150g), trimmed, chopped finely

4cm piece fresh ginger (20g), grated

1 cinnamon stick

100g white medium-grain rice

250ml chicken stock

40g blanched almonds, roasted, chopped finely

2 teaspoons finely grated orange rind

3 medium red peppers (600g)

4 whole rainbow trout (1.2kg)

1 medium orange (240g), peeled, sliced crossways into thin rounds

90g baby spinach

4 tablespoons fresh mint leaves

1 Melt butter in medium saucepan; cook onion, celery, ginger and cinnamon, stirring, about 5 minutes or until vegetables soften. Add rice; cook, stirring, 1 minute. Add stock; bring to the boil. Reduce heat; simmer, covered tightly, over low heat about 12 minutes or until water is absorbed. Remove from heat; stand rice, covered, 10 minutes, cool. Discard cinnamon stick; stir in nuts and rind; season to taste.

2 Meanwhile, preheat oven to 200°C/180°C fan-assisted.

3 Quarter peppers through stems, leaving stem quarters attached to peppers; discard seeds and membranes. Divide pepper quarters between two oiled baking dishes.

4 Fill fish cavities with rice mixture; place fish on peppers. Roast, covered, 20 minutes. Uncover; roast a further 10 minutes or until fish are cooked as desired.

5 Serve fish on pepper; accompany with combined orange, spinach and mint.

prep + cook time 1 hour
serves 4
nutritional count per serving 29g total fat (10.5g saturated fat); 2307kJ (552 cal); 31.5g carbohydrate; 39.3g protein; 5.1g fibre

ROASTED WHITE FISH WITH CHERMOULLA

4 whole baby snapper (1.2kg)
1 teaspoon ground cumin
½ teaspoon hot paprika
2 teaspoons finely grated lemon
  rind
1 tablespoon olive oil

chermoulla
60ml olive oil
4 tablespoons each finely
  chopped fresh flat-leaf parsley
  and coriander
2 tablespoons lemon juice
1 clove garlic, crushed
1 fresh long red chilli, chopped
  finely

1 Preheat oven to 200°C/180°C
fan-assisted. Oil oven tray.
2 Score fish through thickest part
of flesh. Rub fish all over with
combined spices, rind and oil;
season. Place fish on tray; roast,
uncovered, about 25 minutes or
until cooked through.
3 Meanwhile, make chermoulla.
4 Serve fish drizzled with
chermoulla.

chermoulla Combine ingredients
in small bowl; season to taste.

prep + cook time 35 minutes
serves 4
nutritional count per serving
20.8g total fat (3.5g saturated
fat); 1346kJ (322 cal); 0.6g
carbohydrate; 32.6g protein;
0.6g fibre
tip Baby bream or any other firm
white fish would also work well in
this recipe.

ACCOMPANIMENTS

SPICY FRIED POTATOES

1kg baby new potatoes
2 tablespoons olive oil
1 tablespoon harissa
2 cloves garlic, crushed
2 teaspoons cumin seeds
2 teaspoons finely grated lemon
  rind
2 tablespoons finely chopped
  fresh flat-leaf parsley

1 Boil, steam or microwave potatoes until tender; drain, then cut in half.
2 Heat oil in large frying pan; cook potatoes, harissa, garlic and seeds, stirring occasionally, about 10 minutes or until potatoes are browned. Stir in rind and parsley; season to taste.

prep + cook time 35 minutes
serves 6
nutritional count per serving
6.4g total fat (0.9g saturated fat); 732kJ (175 cal); 22.8g carbohydrate; 4.1g protein; 3.8g fibre

MINTED CARROTS WITH GOAT'S CHEESE

1.2kg baby carrots, trimmed
2 tablespoons olive oil
2 tablespoons cumin seeds
1 large handful fresh mint leaves
220g soft goat's cheese,
   crumbled

1 Combine carrots and oil in large bowl; season.
2 Cook carrots on heated oiled grill plate (or grill or barbecue) about 5 minutes or until tender.
3 Meanwhile, dry-fry seeds in small frying pan until fragrant.
4 Combine carrots, seeds, mint and half the cheese in large bowl; sprinkle with remaining cheese.

prep + cook time 35 minutes
serves 6
nutritional count per serving
12.1g total fat (4.7g saturated fat); 769kJ (184 cal); 10g carbohydrate; 6.5g protein; 5.6g fibre
tips We used an ash-coated goat's cheese in the recipe.

FRIED COURGETTES
WITH PINE NUTS & CURRANTS

60ml olive oil

40g butter

2 thick slices ciabatta, crusts removed, chopped finely into cubes

2 cloves garlic, crushed

1 tablespoon roasted pine nuts, chopped coarsely

1 teaspoon finely grated lemon rind

2 tablespoons finely chopped fresh flat-leaf parsley

1 tablespoon currants

24 tiny courgettes with flowers attached

1 Heat half the oil and half the butter in large frying pan, add bread cubes; cook, stirring, until browned lightly. Add garlic; cook, stirring, until fragrant. Stir in nuts, rind, parsley and currants. Transfer to medium bowl; cover to keep warm.

2 Heat remaining oil and butter in same pan, add courgettes; cook, covered, until browned lightly and just tender.

3 Serve courgettes sprinkled with bread mixture.

prep + cook time 30 minutes
serves 8
nutritional count per serving
12g total fat (3.5g saturated fat); 575kJ (137 cal); 5.3g carbohydrate; 1.7g protein; 1.2g fibre
tips The crumb mixture can be made several hours ahead; cook courgettes just before serving. If courgette flowers are not available, substitute small courgettes quartered lengthways.

BEANS WITH TOMATO WALNUT SAUCE

1kg green beans, trimmed
425g canned tomatoes, crushed
1 tablespoon olive oil
2 cloves garlic, crushed
2 teaspoons each ground
    coriander and cumin
¼ teaspoon cayenne pepper
90g coarsely chopped roasted
    walnuts
6 tablespoons coarsely chopped
    fresh coriander
1 teaspoon granulated sugar
1 small red pepper (150g), sliced
    thinly
1 small yellow pepper (150g),
    sliced thinly

1 Boil, steam or microwave beans until tender; drain.

2 Blend or process undrained tomatoes until smooth.

3 Heat oil in large frying pan; cook garlic, spices and nuts, stirring, until fragrant. Add tomatoes, fresh coriander and sugar; cook, stirring, until heated through. Remove from heat, stir in pepper and beans, season to taste.

prep + cook time 25 minutes
serves 6
nutritional count per serving
14g total fat (1.1g saturated fat); 857kJ (205 cal); 9.3g carbohydrate; 7.3g protein; 7.3g fibre

ROASTED VEGETABLE COUSCOUS

1 medium red onion (170g), cut into wedges
4 small courgettes (360g), halved lengthways
10 baby carrots (175g), halved lengthways
2 tablespoons olive oil
200g couscous
250ml boiling water
450g bottled roasted red pepper, drained, sliced thinly
2 tablespoons finely chopped fresh thyme

1 Preheat oven to 220°C/200°C fan-assisted.
2 Combine onion, courgette, carrot and oil in large shallow baking dish; season to taste. Roast, uncovered, about 20 minutes or until vegetables are tender.
3 Combine couscous with the water in large heatproof bowl, cover; stand about 5 minutes or until liquid is absorbed, fluffing with fork occasionally.
4 Stir vegetables and remaining ingredients into couscous; season to taste.

prep + cook time 35 minutes
serves 6
nutritional count per serving
8.3g total fat (1.3g saturated fat); 995kJ (238 cal); 32.1g carbohydrate; 6.7g protein; 3.3g fibre
tip You can use any leftover or store-bought roasted vegetables in this recipe.

PRESERVED LEMON & OLIVE COUSCOUS

250g couscous
310ml boiling water
15g butter
400g canned chickpeas, rinsed,
    drained
60g pitted green olives, chopped
    coarsely
2 tablespoons lemon juice
3 spring onions, sliced thinly
2 tablespoons finely chopped
    fresh flat-leaf parsley
1 tablespoon thinly sliced
    preserved lemon rind

1 Combine couscous with the water and butter in large heatproof bowl, cover; stand about 5 minutes or until water is absorbed, fluffing with fork occasionally.
2 Stir remaining ingredients into couscous; season to taste.

prep time 15 minutes
serves 6
nutritional count per serving
5.3g total fat (1.8g saturated fat); 1020kJ (244 cal); 38.5g carbohydrate; 8.5g protein; 3g fibre

SPICED CAULIFLOWER COUSCOUS

1 tablespoon olive oil

1 small brown onion (80g), sliced thinly

1 teaspoon ground coriander

½ small cauliflower (500g), cut into small florets

2 tablespoons water

4 tablespoons coarsely chopped fresh coriander

250g couscous

310ml boiling water

1 Heat oil in large saucepan; cook onion, stirring, until soft. Add ground coriander and cauliflower; cook, stirring, until fragrant. Add the water; cook, covered, about 10 minutes or until cauliflower is tender and water is absorbed. Stir in half the fresh coriander.

2 Meanwhile, combine couscous with the boiling water in large heatproof bowl, cover; stand about 5 minutes or until liquid is absorbed, fluffing with fork occasionally.

3 Stir cauliflower mixture into couscous; season to taste. Serve sprinkled with remaining fresh coriander.

prep + cook time 25 minutes
serves 6
nutritional count per serving
3.4g total fat (0.5g saturated fat); 844kJ (202 cal); 34.2g carbohydrate; 7.1g protein; 1.9g fibre

SPICY RED COUSCOUS

1 tablespoon olive oil
1 tablespoon harissa
2 teaspoons sweet paprika
4 spring onions, sliced thinly
250ml chicken stock
125ml water
300g couscous
1 tablespoon lemon juice

1 Heat oil in medium saucepan; cook harissa, paprika and half the onion, stirring, about 2 minutes or until fragrant.
2 Add stock and the water to onion mixture; bring to the boil. Remove from heat, add couscous; cover, stand about 5 minutes or until liquid is absorbed, fluffing with fork occasionally.
3 Stir juice into couscous; season to taste. Serve sprinkled with remaining onion.

prep + cook time 15 minutes
serves 6
nutritional count per serving
3.6g total fat (0.6g saturated fat); 928kJ (222 cal); 39.4g carbohydrate; 7g protein; 0.7g fibre

DESSERTS

HAZELNUT & DATE TART

1 sheet shortcrust pastry
125g butter, softened
75g caster sugar
2 tablespoons finely grated
  lemon rind
2 eggs
100g ground hazelnuts
1 tablespoon plain flour
1 teaspoon ground cinnamon
60g pitted dried dates, halved
  lengthways
180g honey, warmed

sesame cream
300ml double cream
2 tablespoons caster sugar
2 teaspoons black sesame seeds
1 teaspoon vanilla extract
1 teaspoon sesame oil

1 Preheat oven to 200°C/180°C
fan-assisted.
2 Line greased 24cm round loose-
based flan tin with pastry; press
into base and sides, trim edge.
Refrigerate 30 minutes.
3 Meanwhile, beat butter, sugar
and rind in small bowl with electric
mixer until combined. Beat in
eggs, one at a time. Stir in ground
hazelnuts, flour and cinnamon.
Spread hazelnut filling into pastry
case; top with dates.
4 Bake tart about 35 minutes or
until firm. Brush hot tart with half
the honey. Cool in tin.
5 Meanwhile, make sesame
cream.
6 Serve tart drizzled with
remaining honey; top with sesame
cream.

sesame cream Beat cream and
sugar in small bowl with electric
mixer until soft peaks form; fold in
remaining ingredients.

prep + cook time 55 minutes
+ refrigeration & cooling time
serves 8
nutritional count per serving
42.6g total fat (21.5g saturated
fat); 2508kJ (600 cal); 49.4g
carbohydrate; 6.5g protein;
2.6g fibre
tip You can use ground almonds
instead of ground hazelnuts if you
prefer.

SAFFRON PANNA COTTA WITH HONEYED FIGS

250ml double cream
110g caster sugar
pinch saffron threads
8 cardamom pods, bruised
2 cinnamon sticks
4 teaspoons gelatine
2 tablespoons water
500ml buttermilk

honeyed figs
90g honey
60ml dry red wine
65g finely chopped dried figs

1 Stir cream, sugar and spices in medium saucepan over low heat until sugar dissolves. Bring to the boil. Strain mixture into large heatproof jug; cool 5 minutes.
2 Meanwhile, sprinkle gelatine over the water in small heatproof jug. Stand jug in small saucepan of simmering water; stir until gelatine dissolves, cool 5 minutes.
3 Stir gelatine mixture and buttermilk into cream mixture. Divide mixture into six 180ml moulds. Cover; refrigerate 4 hours or until set.
4 Make honeyed figs.
5 Turn panna cottas onto serving plates; top with honeyed figs.

honeyed figs Bring ingredients to the boil in medium saucepan. Reduce heat; simmer, uncovered, about 5 minutes or until syrup thickens slightly. Cool.

prep + cook time 30 minutes + refrigeration time
serves 6
nutritional count per serving 19.8g total fat (13g saturated fat); 1576kJ (377 cal); 42.4g carbohydrate; 6.7g protein; 1.5g fibre

WATERMELON & FIG SALAD

1.2kg piece watermelon, seeds removed
6 medium fresh figs (360g), sliced into rounds
200g greek-style yogurt
1 teaspoon rosewater
3 tablespoons fresh small mint leaves
35g roasted walnuts, chopped finely

1 Cut away skin and white pith from melon; cut melon into thin wedges. Arrange melon and figs on serving platter.
2 Combine yogurt and rosewater in small bowl; drizzle over fruit. Sprinkle with mint and nuts.

prep time 15 minutes
serves 4
nutritional count per serving
10.2g total fat (2.7g saturated fat); 882kJ (211 cal); 21.8g carbohydrate; 5.9g protein; 4.2g fibre

ALMOND RICE PUDDING

1.5 litres milk
320g blanched almonds
55g caster sugar
5cm strip orange rind
130g arborio rice
½ teaspoon orange flower water
1 large pomegranate (430g)
35g roasted slivered almonds
pinch ground cinnamon

1 Blend milk and blanched nuts, in batches, until smooth. Strain milk mixture through fine sieve into large saucepan.
2 Stir sugar and rind into milk mixture over high heat; bring to the boil, stirring occasionally. Gradually stir in rice. Reduce heat; simmer, uncovered, over low heat, stirring occasionally, about 35 minutes or until rice is tender. Discard rind; stir in orange flower water. Stand 10 minutes.
3 Remove seeds from pomegranate; serve warm rice sprinkled with seeds, slivered nuts and cinnamon.

prep + cook time 1 hour + standing time
serves 6
nutritional count per serving
42.8g total fat (8.4g saturated fat); 2730kJ (653 cal); 43.5g carbohydrate; 22.4g protein; 6.8g fibre

ROSEWATER & ORANGE COUSCOUS

1 medium orange (240g)
375ml water
75g caster sugar
300g couscous
30g butter
1 teaspoon rosewater
½ teaspoon ground cinnamon
65g finely chopped dried figs
45g coarsely chopped roasted
   unsalted shelled pistachios
190g natural yogurt
3 tablespoons fresh mint leaves

1 Finely grate 2 teaspoons rind from orange. Peel and segment orange over small bowl.
2 Stir the water and sugar in small saucepan over medium heat until sugar dissolves; bring to the boil.
3 Combine couscous with the sugar syrup mixture, butter, rosewater, cinnamon and rind in medium heatproof bowl, cover; stand about 5 minutes or until liquid is absorbed, fluffing with fork occasionally. Stir figs and half the nuts into couscous.
4 Serve couscous topped with orange segments and yogurt; sprinkle with remaining nuts and mint.

prep + cook time 25 minutes + standing time
serves 4
nutritional count per serving
13.5g total fat (5.5g saturated fat); 2362kJ (565 cal); 93.1g carbohydrate; 15.4g protein; 5.1g fibre

ALMOND SHORTBREAD

250g unsalted butter, chopped
1 teaspoon vanilla extract
80g icing sugar, sifted
1 egg yolk
1 tablespoon orange flower water
70g finely chopped toasted
   flaked almonds
300g plain flour
75g self-raising flour
icing sugar, to coat, extra

1 Beat butter, vanilla and sugar in a small bowl with an electric mixer until light and fluffy. Beat in egg yolk and orange flower water. Transfer mixture to a large bowl; stir in almonds and combined sifted flours.
2 Preheat oven to160°C/140°C fan-assisted.
3 Take a level tablespoon of dough and roll between palms into a sausage shape, tapering at ends; bend into a crescent. Repeat with remaining dough. Place on lightly greased baking trays, 3cm apart. Bake for about 15 to 20 minutes or until browned lightly. Cool on baking trays for 5 minutes.
4 Sift a thick layer of the extra icing sugar onto a large sheet of baking parchment. Place shortbreads on icing sugar, dust tops of shortbreads heavily with icing sugar. Cool. Pack into an airtight container, sifting more icing sugar onto each layer. Store at room temperature for up to 1 week.

prep + cook time 50 minutes
makes about 32
nutritional count per shortbread
7.9g total fat (4.4g saturated fat); 523kJ (125 cal); 11g carbohydrate; 1.8g protein; 0.6g fibre

HONEY-COATED PISTACHIO & ROSEWATER PALMIERS

110g roasted unsalted shelled
  pistachios
55g caster sugar
2 teaspoons rosewater
½ teaspoon ground cinnamon
20g butter
2 tablespoons demerara sugar
2 sheets puff pastry
1 egg, beaten lightly
175g honey
1 teaspoon rosewater, extra

1 Blend or process nuts with sugar, rosewater, cinnamon and butter until mixture forms a coarse paste.
2 Sprinkle board with half of the demerara sugar; place one sheet of pastry on the sugar. Using rolling pin, press pastry gently into demerara sugar. Spread half the nut mixture on pastry; fold two opposing sides of the pastry inwards to meet in the middle. Flatten folded pastry slightly; brush with a little of the egg. Fold each side in half to meet in the middle; flatten slightly. Fold the two sides in half again so they just touch in the middle, flattening slightly. Repeat process with remaining demerara sugar, pastry sheet, nut mixture and egg. Cover pastry pieces, separately, with cling film; refrigerate 30 minutes.
3 Meanwhile, preheat oven to 200°C/180°C fan-assisted. Grease oven trays.
4 Cut rolled pastry pieces into 1cm slices; place slices, cut-side up, on trays about 2cm apart.
5 Bake palmiers about 12 minutes or until browned lightly.

6 Meanwhile, bring honey and extra rosewater to the boil in small frying pan. Reduce heat; simmer, uncovered, 3 minutes. Remove from heat.
7 Add hot palmiers, one at a time, to honey mixture, turning to coat all over; drain on greased wire rack. Serve cold.

prep + cook time 45 minutes
+ refrigeration time
makes 32
nutritional count per palmier
4.6g total fat; (0.7g saturated fat); 393kJ (94 cal); 11.5g carbohydrate; 1.4g protein; 0.4g fibre

GAZELLES' HORNS

180g butter, softened
110g icing sugar
2 eggs
400g plain flour
1 tablespoon orange blossom
   water
2 teaspoons iced water,
   approximately
1 tablespoon milk
80g icing sugar, extra
1 teaspoon ground cinnamon

almond filling
240g ground almonds
80g icing sugar
1 egg
45g butter, melted
1 tablespoon orange flower water

1 Beat butter and sifted icing sugar in medium bowl with electric mixer until smooth. Beat in eggs, one at a time. Stir in sifted flour, orange blossom water and enough of the water to make a firm dough. Divide dough in half; cover, refrigerate 30 minutes.
2 Meanwhile, make almond filling.
3 Preheat oven to 160°C/140°C fan-assisted. Grease and line oven trays.
4 Roll each dough half, separately, between sheets of baking parchment until 2mm thick; cut 20 x 7.5cm rounds from each sheet of dough. Re-roll scraps of dough, if necessary, to make a total of 40 rounds.
5 Drop rounded teaspoons of almond filling into centre of rounds; brush edges with a little water. Fold rounds in half, press edges with a fork to seal. Pinch ends slightly to create horn shapes. Place horns on oven trays; brush with milk. Bake about 20 minutes or until browned lightly.

6 Roll warm horns in combined extra sifted icing sugar and cinnamon. Horns can be served warm or cold.

almond filling Combine ingredients in medium bowl.

prep + cook time 1 hour
+ refrigeration time
makes 40
nutritional count per horn
8.5g total fat (3.4g saturated fat); 606kJ (145 cal); 14.3g carbohydrate; 2.9g protein; 0.9g fibre

GLOSSARY

allspice also known as pimento or Jamaican pepper; available whole or ground.

anchovies small saltwater fish; they are filleted, salted, matured and packed in oil or brine, giving them a characteristic strong taste. Available canned or in jars, they are used in small quantities to flavour a variety of dishes

arborio rice small, round-grain rice; especially suitable for risottos.

artichoke hearts tender centre of the globe artichoke; purchased in brine canned or in jars.

avocado oil pressed from the flesh of the avocado fruit, this oil has a high smoking point and is high in monounsaturated fats and vitamin E.

buttermilk fresh low-fat milk cultured to give a slightly sour, tangy taste; low-fat yogurt or milk can be substituted.

caraway seeds a member of the parsley family; available in seed or ground form.

cardamom can be bought in pod, seed or ground form. Has a distinctive, aromatic, sweetly rich flavour.

chermoulla a Moroccan blend of fresh herbs, spices and condiments, chermoulla is traditionally used for preserving or seasoning meat and fish.

ciabatta meaning 'slipper' in Italian, the traditional shape of this popular crisp-crusted white bread.

cinnamon dried inner bark of the shoots of the cinnamon tree. Available as a stick or ground.

consommé a clear soup usually made of beef, veal or chicken.

coriander also known as cilantro or chinese parsley; bright-green-leafed herb with a fragrant, pungent flavour. Dried coriander seeds and ground coriander are also available. These must never be used to replace fresh coriander or vice versa; the tastes are completely different.

couscous a fine, grain-like cereal product, made from semolina.

cumin available both ground and as whole seeds; cumin has a warm, earthy, rather strong flavour.

date fruit of the date palm tree, eaten fresh or dried, on their own or in prepared dishes. About 4cm to 6cm in length, oval and plump, thin-skinned, with a honey-sweet flavour and sticky texture.

feta cheese a crumbly textured goat's- or sheep's-milk cheese with a sharp, salty taste.

filo pastry chilled or frozen tissue-thin pastry sheets that are very versatile, lending themselves to both sweet and savoury dishes.

gelatine we used powdered gelatine; also available in sheet form known as leaf gelatine.

ginger
fresh also called green or root ginger; the thick gnarled root of a tropical plant. Can be kept, peeled, covered with dry sherry in a jar and refrigerated, or frozen in an airtight container.

ground also called powdered ginger; cannot be substituted for fresh ginger.

harissa a North African spicy paste made from dried red chillies, garlic, olive oil and caraway seeds. It can be used as a rub for meat, an ingredient in sauces and dressings, or eaten on its own as a condiment. It is available, ready-made, from Middle-Eastern food shops and most supermarkets.

olives

black have a richer and more mellow flavour than the green ones and are softer in texture.
green olives harvested before fully ripened and are, as a rule, denser and more bitter than their black relatives.

onions

brown and white onions are interchangeable. Their pungent flesh adds flavour to a vast range of dishes.
red also known as spanish; a sweet-flavoured, large, purple-red onion.

orange flower water concentrated flavouring made from orange blossoms. Cannot be substituted with citrus flavourings, as the taste is completely different.

paprika ground dried red pepper (capsicum); available sweet, smoked or hot.

pine nuts also known as pignoli; small, cream-coloured kernels obtained from the cones of different varieties of pine trees.

pitta bread a slightly leavened, soft, flat bread. When baked, the bread puffs up, leaving a hollow, like a pocket, which can then be stuffed with savoury fillings. Pitta is also eaten with dips or soups, or toasted to form the basis of fattoush.

plum sauce a thick, sweet and sour dipping sauce made from plums, vinegar, sugar, chillies and spices.

poppy seeds small, dried, bluish-grey seeds of the poppy plant with a crunchy texture and a nutty flavour. Available whole or ground in most supermarkets.

preserved lemon a North African specialty, lemons are preserved, usually whole, in a mixture of salt and lemon juice or oil. To use, remove and discard pulp, squeeze juice from rind, then rinse rind well before slicing thinly. Available from specialty food shops, delicatessens and good supermarkets.

prunes commercially or sun-dried plums.

ras el hanout a classic Moroccan spice blend often containing more than 20 different spices. The name means 'top of the shop' and is the very best spice blend that a spice merchant has to offer.

rocket also known as arugula, rugula and rucola; a peppery-tasting green leaf.

rosewater extract made from crushed rose petals; available from health food stores, speciality grocers and good supermarkets.

saffron one of the most expensive spices in the world, true saffron comes only from the saffron crocus, that can produce several flowers a year.

sesame oil made from roasted, crushed, white sesame seeds; a flavouring rather than a cooking medium.

sesame seeds both white and black sesame seeds are available. Black sesame seeds are available at healthfood stores and online.

sugar

brown an extremely soft, fine granulated sugar retaining molasses for its deep colour and flavour.
caster also known as superfine or finely granulated table sugar.
demerara small-grained golden-coloured crystal sugar.
granulated we used coarse table sugar, unless otherwise specified.
icing also known as confectioners' sugar or powdered sugar.

turmeric a member of the ginger family, its root is dried and ground; intensely pungent in taste but not hot.

vanilla extract obtained from vanilla pods infused in water; a non-alcoholic version of vanilla essence.

za'atar a blend of roasted sesame seeds, sumac and crushed dried herbs such as wild marjoram and thyme, its content is largely determined by the individual maker. Used to flavour many familiar Middle Eastern dishes, pizza and savoury pastries; available in delicatessens, specialty food stores and good supermarkets.

INDEX

A

almonds
    almond harissa roast lamb 75
    almond rice pudding 115
    almond shortbread 119
    beef, raisin & almond tagine 53
    gazelles' horns 123
    roast trout with orange almond filling 84
artichokes: lamb, artichoke & pepper tagine 42
aubergines
    aubergine dip 10
    beef & aubergine tagine 50

B

beans with tomato walnut sauce 97
beef
    beef & aubergine tagine 50
    beef & fig cigars 14
    beef, raisin & almond tagine 53
    meatball tagine with eggs 49
beetroot: roasted pepper & beetroot salad 35
biscuits
    almond shortbread 119
    gazelles' horns 123

C

cannellini beans: white bean & lentil tagine 65
carrots
    carrot, raisin & herb salad 36
    minted carrots with goat's cheese 93
cauliflower couscous, spiced 102
chermoulla, roasted white fish with 87
chicken
    chicken tagine with olives & lemon 54
    chicken tagine with prunes & honey 57

chicken with couscous stuffing 80
citrus chicken with orange & pistachio couscous 79
roasted harissa chicken 83
rosewater & sesame chicken drumsticks 22
chickpeas: goat's cheese with chickpeas & peppers 21
chilli fish tagine 61
citrus chicken with orange & pistachio couscous 79
courgettes with pine nuts & currants, fried 94
couscous
    chicken with couscous stuffing 80
    citrus chicken with orange & pistachio couscous 79
    preserved lemon & olive couscous 101
    roasted vegetable couscous 98
    rosewater & orange couscous 116
    spiced cauliflower couscous 102
    spicy red couscous 105
cucumbers
    cucumber & feta salad with za'atar 28
    radish & cucumber chopped salad 39
    sweet cucumber & orange salad 31
currants: fried courgettes with pine nuts & currants 94

D

dates: hazelnut & date tart 108
dips
    aubergine 10
    red pepper 13

E

eggs, meatball tagine with 49

F

feta: cucumber & feta salad with za'atar 28
figs
    beef & fig cigars 14
    chicken tagine with figs & walnuts 58
    saffron panna cotta with honeyed figs 111
    spiced lamb roast with figs & honey 72
    watermelon & fig salad 112
fish
    chilli fish tagine 61
    minted tuna triangles 18
    roast trout with orange almond filling 84
    roasted white fish with chermoulla 87

G

gazelles' horns 123
goat's cheese
    goat's cheese with chickpeas & peppers 21
    minted carrots with goat's cheese 93

H

harissa
    almond harissa roast lamb 75
    roasted harissa chicken 83
    vegetarian cigars with harissa yogurt 17
hazelnuts: hazelnut & date tart 108
herbs
    carrot, raisin & herb salad 36
    salad of herbs 32
honey
    chicken tagine with prunes & honey 57
    honey-coated pistachio & rosewater palmiers 120

saffron panna cotta with honeyed figs 111

spiced lamb roast with figs & honey 72

L

lamb
almond harissa roast lamb 75
lamb, artichoke & pepper tagine 42
lamb kebabs with yogurt & pitta bread 25
lamb tagine with ras el hanout 46
lamb tagine with sweet prunes 45
slow-roasted spiced lamb shoulder 76
spiced lamb roast with figs & honey 72
lemons see preserved lemons
lentils: white bean & lentil tagine 65

M

meatball tagine with eggs 49
mint
minted carrots with goat's cheese 93
minted tuna triangles 18

O

olives
chicken tagine with olives & lemon 54
preserved lemon & olive couscous 101
oranges
citrus chicken with orange & pistachio couscous 79
roast trout with orange almond filling 84
rosewater & orange couscous 116
sweet cucumber & orange salad 31

P

palmiers, honey-coated pistachio & rosewater 120
panna cotta: saffron panna cotta with honeyed figs 111

pastries
beef & fig cigars 14
honey-coated pistachio & rosewater palmiers 120
minted tuna triangles 18
vegetarian cigars 17
peppers
goat's cheese with chickpeas & peppers 21
lamb, artichoke & pepper tagine 42
red pepper dip 13
roasted pepper & beetroot salad 35
pine nuts: fried courgettes with pine nuts & currants 94
pistachios
citrus chicken with orange & pistachio couscous 79
honey-coated pistachio & rosewater palmiers 120
pitta bread, lamb kebabs with yogurt & 25
potatoes, spicy fried 90
prawns: spicy prawn & tomato tagine 62
preserved lemons
chicken tagine with olives & lemon 54
preserved lemon & olive couscous 101
prunes
chicken tagine with prunes & honey 57
lamb tagine with sweet prunes 45

R

radish & cucumber chopped salad 39
raisins
beef, raisin & almond tagine 53
carrot, raisin & herb salad 36
ras el hanout, lamb tagine with 46
rice pudding, almond 115
rosewater
honey-coated pistachio & rosewater palmiers 120

rosewater & orange couscous 116
rosewater & sesame chicken drumsticks 22

S

saffron panna cotta with honeyed figs 111
sesame seeds: rosewater & sesame chicken drumsticks 22
shortbread, almond 119
split peas, vegetable tagine with 69

T

tart, hazelnut & date 108
tomatoes
beans with tomato walnut sauce 97
spicy prawn & tomato tagine 62
trout with orange almond filling, roast 84
tuna: minted tuna triangles 18

V

vegetables
roasted vegetable couscous 98
sweet & spicy vegetable tagine 66
vegetable tagine with split peas 69
vegetarian cigars with harissa yogurt 17

W

walnuts
beans with tomato walnut sauce 97
chicken tagine with figs & walnuts 58
watermelon & fig salad 112
white bean & lentil tagine 65

Y

yogurt
lamb kebabs with yogurt & pitta bread 25
vegetarian cigars with harissa yogurt 17

Z

za'atar, cucumber & feta salad with 28

CONVERSION CHARTS

measures

One metric tablespoon holds 20ml; one metric teaspoon holds 5ml.

All cup and spoon measurements are level. The most accurate way of measuring dry ingredients is to weigh them. When measuring liquids, use a clear glass or plastic jug with metric markings.

We use large eggs with an average weight of 60g.

dry measures

METRIC	IMPERIAL
15g	½oz
30g	1oz
60g	2oz
90g	3oz
125g	4oz (¼lb)
155g	5oz
185g	6oz
220g	7oz
250g	8oz (½lb)
280g	9oz
315g	10oz
345g	11oz
375g	12oz (¾lb)
410g	13oz
440g	14oz
470g	15oz
500g	16oz (1lb)
750g	24oz (1½lb)
1kg	32oz (2lb)

liquid measures

METRIC	IMPERIAL
30ml	1 fluid oz
60ml	2 fluid oz
100ml	3 fluid oz
125ml	4 fluid oz
150ml	5 fluid oz
190ml	6 fluid oz
250ml	8 fluid oz
300ml	10 fluid oz
500ml	16 fluid oz
600ml	20 fluid oz
1000ml (1 litre)	32 fluid oz

length measures

3mm	⅛in
6mm	¼in
1cm	½in
2cm	¾in
2.5cm	1in
5cm	2in
6cm	2½in
8cm	3in
10cm	4in
13cm	5in
15cm	6in
18cm	7in
20cm	8in
23cm	9in
25cm	10in
28cm	11in
30cm	12in (1ft)

oven temperatures

These are fan-assisted temperatures. If you have a conventional oven (ie. not fan-assisted), increase temperatures by 10–20°.

	°C (CELSIUS)	°F (FAHRENHEIT)	GAS MARK
Very low	100	210	½
Low	130	260	1–2
Moderately low	140	280	3
Moderate	160	325	4–5
Moderately hot	180	350	6
Hot	200	400	7–8
Very hot	220	425	9